Chester River Adventist School
305 N. Kent Street
Chestertown, MD 21620

AMAZING WORKING DOGS with

AMERICAN HUMANE
Protecting Children & Animals Since 1877

SEARCH AND RESCUE DOG HEROES

Linda Bozzo

Bailey Books
an imprint of
Enslow Publishers, Inc.
40 Industrial Road
Box 398
Berkeley Heights, NJ 07922
USA
http://www.enslow.com

Founded in 1877, the American Humane Association is the only national organization dedicated to protecting both children and animals. Through a network of child and animal protection agencies and individuals, American Humane develops policies, legislation, curricula, and training programs—and takes action—to protect children and animals from abuse, neglect, and exploitation. To learn how you can support American Humane's vision of a nation where no child or animal will ever be a victim of abuse or neglect, visit www.americanhumane.org, phone (303) 792-9900, or write to the American Humane Association at 63 Inverness Drive East, Englewood, Colorado, 80112-5117.

AMERICAN HUMANE

Protecting Children & Animals Since 1877

Dedication

This book is dedicated to Lieutenant Mitch Ellicott and to the memory of his K-9, Radar.

Thank You

The author would like to thank Lieutenant Mitch Ellicott for being so generous with his time and knowledge. She would also like to thank him for sharing his new K-9 Blaze as well his passion for all of his dogs. The author would also like to thank her dad for tagging along and sharing this wonderful experience.

Enslow Publishers, Inc. wishes to thank James Culpepper, Co-owner of Lead K-9 and Vice President of the American Working Dog Association for reviewing this book.

Bailey Books, an imprint of Enslow Publishers, Inc.

Copyright © 2011 by Enslow Publishers, Inc.

Library of Congress Cataloging-in-Publication Data

Bozzo, Linda.
    Search and rescue dog heroes / Linda Bozzo.
        p. cm. — (Amazing working dogs with American Humane)
    Includes bibliographical references and index.
    Summary: "The text opens with a true story of a search and rescue (SAR) dog, and then it explains the history of the SAR K-9 team and the training methods used to transform an ordinary dog into a canine hero"—Provided by publisher.
    ISBN-13: 978-0-7660-3201-9
    ISBN-10: 0-7660-3201-9
    1. Search dogs—Juvenile literature. 2. Rescue dogs—Juvenile literature. I. Title.
SF428.73.B69 2010
636.7'0886—dc22   2008048018

Printed in China

052010 Leo Paper Group, Heshan City, Guangdong, China.

10 9 8 7 6 5 4 3 2 1

To Our Readers: We have done our best to make sure all Internet Addresses in this book were active and appropriate when we went to press. However, the author and the publisher have no control over and assume no liability for the material available on those Internet sites or on other Web sites they may link to. Any comments or suggestions can be sent by e-mail to comments@enslow.com or to the address on the back cover.

Every effort has been made to locate all copyright holders of material used in this book. If any errors or omissions have occurred, corrections will be made in future editions of this book.

Illustration Credits: Associated Press, pp. 14, 22, 32, 38; Ashley Cooper/Corbis, p. 35; John Degutis, p. 46; Courtesy of Mitchell Ellicott, pp. 4, 7, 9; © Hulton-Deutsch Collection/Corbis, p. 13; © 2009 Jupiterimages Corporation, p. 44; Courtesy of Officer Lim, p. 39; Lawrence Migdale/Photo Researchers, Inc., p. 41; Pearcy, Robert/Animals Animals-Earth Scenes, pp. 1, 30; © David Pollack/K.J. Historical/Corbis, p. 12; The Rooms Provincial Archives, NA 1534, p. 11; Search Dog Foundation, pp. 25, 28; Shutterstock, pp. 17, 18, 19, 42.

Cover Illustration: Pearcy, Robert/Animals Animals-Earth Scenes.

Contents

Here Radar performs a
training exercise. Radar is
sniffing the car for drugs.

Radar

A True Story

It is a cool evening in early June. A teenage boy in Sussex County, New Jersey, decides it is perfect weather to ride his BMX bike. He heads for the nearby state park, where dirt trails are rocky and steep. They twist and turn in all directions. What the boy does not know is that not all of the trails are clearly marked. Some are not even part of the park system. After a while, the trails all start to look the same to the boy. He becomes confused. The sun begins to dip behind the trees. He worries that he may be lost. The teenager notices that his cell-phone battery is getting weaker. His worry turns to fear. Alarmed, he calls 911 for help.

"Stay in one place," the police officer tells him. "We will try to find you." The police attempt to track the boy's cell phone, but their attempt is not successful. Police hover overhead in a helicopter, but the leaves from the trees block their view. They decide to call for more help.

It is 9:30 P.M. and darkness has fallen. Sergeant Mitch Ellicott, from the Sussex County sheriff's office, receives a call.

"We need Radar's help," the police officer tells him. "We have a fifteen year old boy lost in the state park."

Radar is Sergeant Ellicott's search and rescue dog. Radar is a German shepherd.

During a training exercise, Radar runs through the forest.

"We will be right there," Sergeant Ellicott tells the officer.

Sergeant Ellicott checks his map of the park. He locates the general area where the boy was last spoken to before his cell phone lost power. The area to be searched is decided. A search team is put together.

The official search begins as a full moon lights the night sky.

Holding Radar by the collar, Sergeant Ellicott yells as loud as he can. "This is the police. I have a search and rescue dog. We are coming to find you." Then in a whisper he asks Radar, "Where's the lost person?" Radar is released. He scouts ahead of the team.

Meanwhile, the boy is scared and panics. Instead of staying in one place, he tries to find his way out. He falls down crossing a stream. Luckily, he is not badly hurt. He heads farther up into the mountain. This makes the search more difficult.

Down below, Radar never stops sniffing. With his head lifted, Radar sniffs the air. This is how he searches for the boy's scent. It is his keen sense of smell that helps him find people. After several hours of searching, Sergeant Ellicott and the other officers hear Radar up ahead, barking. This is Radar's way of letting them

During the training exercise, Radar found him! Radar is truly a hero.

know he has found either something or someone. They are relieved to discover he has found the lost boy.

Wet and muddy from falling in the stream, the boy is happy to see Radar and the police officers. Radar has done his job as a search and rescue dog. Sergeant Ellicott tells Radar, "Good boy." He hugs his dog and pats him on the head. Radar licks him back. Radar is a true canine hero.

Chapter 1

The History of Search and Rescue Dogs

 ogs have a natural ability to hunt. That is why throughout history dogs have proved to be successful in search and rescue work.

There was a time when Newfoundland dogs were known for their work in water rescue. They had a history of pulling sailors to shore, saving them from drowning. Today's water recovery dogs have a much different job. Today, dogs of all breeds help divers locate drowned victims.

Sable Chief, a Newfoundland, was a mascot for the Newfoundland Regiment in World War I.

In the 1900s, during World War I, dogs were trained to help find wounded soldiers on the battlefield. They sniffed human scents in the air to track the victims much like dogs do today.

Disaster dogs got their start during World War II. The military trained dogs to help locate victims buried in fallen buildings. Due to their success, rescuers all over the world began to realize the value of dogs to help find lost or trapped victims.

Dogs were trained to search for people buried in avalanches or fallen ice or snow in the Swiss Alps.

This poster is trying to get men to enlist in the Army during World War I.

Depending on how deep the snow is, the human scent can travel through the snow until it reaches the surface where the dog can smell it. This method of finding victims proved to be more successful than previous methods.

The use of rescue dogs spread to America in the late 1970s. Search and rescue teams could be found on the

These two dogs trained with the Finnish Army in 1940.

scene of building or wilderness searches for people. They proved to be successful in locating lost and missing people.

In more recent years, dogs have played key roles in the recovery of victims of disasters. When the Alfred P. Murrah Federal Building in Oklahoma City was bombed on the morning of April 19, 1995, emergency people and volunteers arrived on the scene. After searching for more than thirteen days, dogs successfully found fifty bodies.

Tornadoes ripped through Oklahoma in 1999.

This search and rescue dog and his handler search a home destroyed by Hurricane Katrina in 2005.

Dogs were used to search for victims of this natural disaster. That same year, search and rescue dogs appeared on the scene when Hurricane Floyd hit.

Hundreds of dogs and their handlers, known as K-9 teams, from around the country arrived in response to the fallen towers of the World Trade Center on September 11, 2001. K-9 teams worked long hours until the list of the missing became shorter and shorter.

Then on August 29, 2005, Hurricane Katrina came ashore in New Orleans, Louisiana. Thousands of people and hundreds of animals are alive today due to the efforts of many search and rescue teams.

Search and rescue is just one of the many jobs dogs perform. They continue to be heroes to many communities around the world. Today, as in the past, thousands of search and rescue dogs, along with their handlers, continue to work to save lives.

Chapter 2

Search and Rescue Dog Breeds

A search and rescue (SAR) dog is trained to find human scent. This specially trained dog uses human scent to find lost or missing people.

Popular breed choices for search and rescue work are German shepherds, golden retrievers, and Labrador retrievers, to name a few. Over the years, these breeds have proven themselves to be successful in search and rescue.

These breeds are usually medium to large in size. SAR dogs should be large enough to handle all kinds of terrain, or surfaces of land. At the same time, they should be small enough so the handler can lift or assist them when necessary. These breeds are also known to be friendly and work well with people.

One popular breed of SAR dog is the German shepherd.

That is what these dogs do. Search and rescue dogs work hard to find people.

But SAR dogs are not limited to any specific breed. Dogs of all types have shown success in search and rescue work. More important than the breed, is the dog's ability to perform its job of finding and rescuing people.

Search and rescue dogs need to be smart. They must be able to obey commands from their handler. Search and rescue dogs should love to work. They

Golden retrievers also make good search and rescue dogs.

may often work long hours. These energetic dogs must also love to play. Playtime is often their reward for search and rescue work. Dogs have a keen sense of smell. But a dog with a long nose, like a Labrador, is better able to detect scent. Both male and female dogs make good search partners.

Another type of dog that makes a good search and rescue dog is the Labrador retriever.

There are many things to consider when choosing a dog. Most important, the person who is handling the dog should choose a breed he or she feels most comfortable working with. After all, they will be a team. Handlers and their dogs will be together for many years.

Chapter 3

K-9 Team Search and Rescue Training

ogs and the people who handle them must learn basic search and rescue skills. Classes can take place at a training center with a certified trainer. It is the trainer's job to prepare the Search and Rescue (SAR) K-9 team to perform search and rescue work.

The SAR K-9 Team

The SAR K-9 team is made up of the search and rescue

dog handlers and their dogs. The search and rescue dogs are carefully trained and tested. The dogs must always be able to follow their handlers' commands.

Search and Rescue Handlers

A search and rescue dog handler is the person who owns and trains the search and rescue dog. Sometimes the handler is a police officer. Sometimes the handler is a volunteer. Either way, the handler is responsible for the care of his or her dog.

Handlers interested in performing search and rescue work must like working with dogs. They must be able to answer a call for help at any time. Searches can take place day or night. Handlers should enjoy working outdoors. They will be expected to work in all kinds of weather.

It is important for handlers to be in good physical shape. After all, they will need to keep up with the

22

search dog. Sometimes searches can take place over long distances. Sometimes the terrain is rough. Handlers should also be strong enough to assist their dogs over an obstacle, like a fence.

SAR dog handlers are trained on how to use a map and a compass. These tools are used to guide them during a search. First-aid training is a must for search and rescue work. Remember, a successful search can turn into a rescue. The handler cares for the person until medical help arrives. Training in animal first aid is necessary as well in case the dog becomes injured.

The handler is trained in radio communications. Communicating with other members of the search team is important. Outdoor survival skills are also taught. Handlers must be prepared to take care of themselves and their dogs overnight if needed.

This dog and his handler are training at a ski area in Colorado. If there is an avalanche, the dog may be called in to help find any stranded people.

Search and Rescue Dogs

Some basic skills are required from dogs as well. Search and rescue dogs are trained to move quickly and easily. Agility training includes climbing, jumping, balancing, and walking over different types of terrain. Search dogs will train in all kinds of weather, including rain and snow.

These dogs are taught to be social animals. They are taken to places like stores and parks. This helps them get comfortable around people and other dogs. They also learn to work around loud noises, like shouting and sirens, without being frightened.

During training, a search dog learns to obey commands given by his or her handler. Some simple commands include *down*, *sit*, *stay*, *heel*, and *come*. A search dog learns to move slowly and carefully when needed. Searching an area needs to be done with care.

For safety, search dogs are trained to approach an unsafe area, like a burned building, carefully.

SAR dogs can be trained to perform different kinds of work. Some dogs are trained to do cadaver searches. This means searching for human remains above or below the ground. Dogs can also be trained in disaster search. They search for people who are victims of a natural or human-caused disaster. This includes floods and fallen buildings.

Training is very important for the dogs and their handlers. The dogs must get along with other people and other dogs.

Some dogs are even trained in water search. They search for people who have drowned. Imagine a dog that searches for people in snowstorms or those buried in avalanches. These dogs are trained to search beneath the snow for people.

Dogs trained in article search learn to find items that may be clues. This can be a shoe or a jacket the person was wearing. These clues can help find the lost or missing person.

Training

Search and rescue training begins after the handler chooses a dog. Most often, dogs chosen are puppies. Puppies are sometimes adopted from a shelter. Some people prefer to train puppies purchased from breeders. Either way, puppies can usually begin training as early as seven to eight weeks old.

The SAR dog and the handler attend group training

sessions with a trainer. But that is not all. Dog and handler also need to do their homework. They need to practice their lessons. A gentle but firm voice should be used when training a dog. The dog should see training exercises as fun. Rewards of praise, playtime, or food are used when teaching a dog.

The handler needs to be patient. Dogs may need to repeat exercises until they get them right. Training a search and rescue dog takes lots of practice. That training never ends as long as the dog and handler are working together.

Passing the Test

To become a SAR K-9 team, the handler and dog need to pass a series of tests. These tests measure the ability of the dog and the handler. Once they have passed, the SAR K-9 team can begin its work with police agencies. The SAR K-9 team will help search for and rescue lost or missing people.

After training, the dog and handler must pass a series of tests.

Even after they have passed the tests, training continues for the dog and his handler. They will continue to train and retest throughout their career as a SAR K-9 team.

Chapter 4

Search and Rescue Dogs on the Job

Search and rescue (SAR) K-9 teams work with rescue squads, police departments, and fire companies. Most often they help search for lost or missing people. A lost person can be a child who got separated from his or her parents. A missing person can be an elderly person who has wandered away from home.

Getting Ready

When on the job, a SAR dog may wear a flat collar with an identification tag. Most SAR dogs also wear a vest and harness when working. This signals to the dog that it is time to work. Booties may protect a dog's paws in rough terrain like rocks or snow. During disaster searches, SAR dogs do not wear anything that can get caught on metal or rocks. This will help keep them from getting hurt.

When on the job, SAR dogs may wear a special vest.

The SAR K-9 team's job begins when it is called by law enforcement. The SAR team must respond immediately. At the scene, they are met by other members of the search team. More than one SAR K-9 team can work at the same time. Each team covers an area. The search starts in the last place the missing person or victim was known to be. It is the SAR K-9 team's job to help locate the person or find clues that will lead to him or her.

How Search Dogs Work

Dogs are valued in search and rescue because of their keen sense of smell. They can smell things that people cannot. Each person has his or her own individual scent. Dogs can smell the difference between those scents. There are several ways a dog uses scent to search.

Air Scent Dogs

When there is no trail to follow, air scent dogs locate human scent as it travels through the air. People shed dead skin cells. A group of skin cells is called a raft. These rafts are carried by the air and wind. Each raft

This handler leads his dog through a building collapse. The dog is sniffing for bodies.

carries the scent of that person. With their heads lifted high, air scent dogs follow the scent of rafts off lead, or not attached to a leash. This allows the dog to run ahead.

Trailing Dogs

Trailing dogs follow a person's scent left along the ground. They will follow the human scent wherever it drifts, often a distance from the trail. Trailing dogs are often given a scent article to smell. A scent article is an item that has the person's scent on it, like a piece of clothing. The dog sniffs for the person's individual scent. The trailing dog is started on the trail at a point where the person was last seen.

Tracking Dogs

Tracking dogs, on the other hand, follow scents left on the path by the person. By sniffing the ground walked on by the person, the dog follows his or her footsteps. Tracking dogs stay close to the person's actual path. Tracking dogs follow the person's exact path, whereas trailing dogs may drift across the path or cut corners for a faster search.

Most trailing and tracking dogs work in a harness with a lead, or long leash. Some work off lead. Once the person is found, some dogs stay with him or her and bark. The handler will follow the sound of the dog's bark to locate the person. Other dogs are trained to return to the handler when the person is found. The dog then takes the handler back to her find. This is called a refind.

The Search and Rescue

Search and rescue jobs can last all night or even days. The handler carries a backpack with supplies for both the handler and the dog. The SAR K-9 team continues searching the area until the person is found or the

Sometimes a search and rescue job needs a helicopter. This dog is wearing his bright orange vest and is ready to begin his job.

search is called off. A search can be called off if the area becomes too dangerous for the team. A search team's hope is that the person will be found and returned safely to his or her loved ones.

At the end of a search, dogs are usually rewarded with food or a toy and playtime. Praise is also important for these hardworking dogs. Search and rescue dogs relate searching for people and their clues to being fun. That is why they love to work!

Retiring

There will come a time when the search and rescue dog will need to retire, or no longer work. A working dog retires when it can no longer perform its job. This may be due to an illness or injury. In most cases, the search and rescue dog will live the rest of its life with its handler as a member of his or her family.

Chapter 5

Search and Rescue Dogs Are Heroes

ay after day, search and rescue dogs save lives in communities everywhere. They love the job they do. It could be a wilderness search where a lost child is found. It could be saving victims of natural disasters like floods or hurricanes. Finding a person buried in an avalanche or under rubble takes skill. These animals are able to cover areas faster than humans can. They are able to smell things that humans cannot.

Search and rescue dogs are very special dogs and are heroes.

No one knows when a search and rescue dog may be needed. They must be ready at all times to answer a call for help. Search and rescue dogs can make a difference between life and death. Ready at all times, these dogs are brave. They make our world a safer place to live. That is why search and rescue dogs are heroes.

K-9 Sirius and his handler, Officer Lim, were on scene after the collapse of the World Trade Center towers on September 11, 2001.

Chapter 6

Safety Tips

 efore you go anywhere—be sure to tell your parents or a trusted adult. Never go into the woods without a buddy. Stay on paths or marked trails when hiking. Even with an adult you could get lost. If someone you know has a GPS (Global Positioning System) ask if you can take it with you. If you have a cell phone, always make sure it is fully charged. You never know when you will need it. Sometimes people in a group can even become separated. These things can happen. But do not worry.

People will start to look for you once they realize you are missing. Here are some tips that will help searchers find you.

Call for Help

Use your cell phone to call 911 for help. Do not wait. Waiting can result in the battery of the cell phone losing power. The more time that passes, the more difficult it could be to find you. It could become dark or it could start to rain. This makes searching harder.

Before you go for a hike, be sure to tell your parents or a trusted adult. Don't forget a map and compass or GPS!

Stay Calm

Try not to panic. People will be looking for you. If you hear people yelling your name, do not be scared. They are not mad at you. They are just trying to find you. Be sure to answer them. Call out for help as loud as you can so searchers can hear you. Calling out or blowing a whistle three times lets people know you need help.

Make sure you are prepared for your hike. Carry a backpack with food and water.

Stay Put

Once you have found a safe place, stay there. Moving around will only get you more lost. It also makes it more difficult for searchers to find you.

Moving around could even cause you to fall and injure yourself.

Keep Warm and Dry

Stay away from water like lakes or streams so you will not get wet. If it is raining, find shelter under a tree or next to a large rock. Use anything you may have to keep you warm and dry. If you are with a friend, you can huddle together to keep warm.

Help Searchers See You

Choose to stay in a place where searchers can see you. A good place to wait is under a large tree. However, if you hear a helicopter overhead find a clearing and lie down. It is easier for people to see you from the air if you are lying on the ground. Wave your arms and legs. You can even spell something the searchers can see. You can draw in the dirt or use rocks or sticks to spell H-E-L-P. Hang brightly colored clothing from a

Hiking is great for the whole family. Keep everyone safe by always knowing where each family member is.

high branch or spread it on the ground for searchers to spot.

The idea is to stay safe while waiting for help to arrive. By remembering these important tips, you will help searchers find you as quickly as possible.

Glossary

article search—Search for an article, such as a piece of clothing, that may contain human scent.

avalanche—A large mass of snow or ice sliding down a mountain.

breed—A certain type of dog

cadaver search—Search for human remains on or below ground.

disaster search—Search for humans after a disaster, such as a hurricane or fallen building.

off lead—When a dog is not attached to a leash.

raft—A group of human skin cells.

refind—When a dog finds a person or article and then leads the handler back to the find.

rubble—Rough or broken things like stones or bricks.

scent article—An item that was recently worn by the victim, such as a piece of clothing.

terrain—The surface features of the land.

water search—Search under the water for humans who have drowned.

After Radar died in 2008, Mitch Ellicott, now a lieutenant, partnered with a new dog, Blaze. The author feels very lucky to have met Lieutenant Ellicott and his K-9.

Further Reading

Books

Jackson, Donna M. *Hero Dogs: Courageous Canines in Action*. New York: Little, Brown, 2003.

Miller, Marie-Therese. *Distinguished Dogs*. New York: Chelsea Clubhouse, 2007.

O'Sullivan, Robyn. *More Than Man's Best Friend: The Story of Working Dogs*. Washington, D.C.: National Geographic, 2006.

Internet Addresses

American Humane Association
http://www.americanhumane.org

American Kennel Club
http://www.akc.org/kids_juniors/

FEMA Federal Emergency Management Agency
http://www.fema.gov/kids/index.htm

Index